Theaters of War

Theaters of War

Emmanuel K. Ngwainmbi

Plain View Press
P. O. 42255
Austin, TX 78704

plainviewpress.net
sbright1@austin.rr.com
1-512-440-7139

Cover Art: *Battlefield*, © Tunde Afoloyana, 2006 —
www. tundevisualart.com

Contents

Scene II: 51

Scene III: 75

"Whatever you do, do it well, for its content and consequence complement its cause."
—E. Ngwainmbi

Scene I:

Hannah and Bill

My Dear Hannah

The gunshots have paused.
I must finish this letter
before our platoon leaves.

I don't know where we'll be going.
I don't when or
if I'll be back.

If my breath expires,
tell Jane and Dempsey I did this so they could grow up
proud to be born in the Land of the Free.

If my body returns home
bring me only plastic flowers
so they can stay fresh until you return.

To Bill, Platoon 545000, Basra, Iraq: Return Receipt Requested

My Dear Bill:

You do not die alone.
You die with your lily
blooming in our flowerbed.

Water it
and moisten my fears
and the g.

Come.

Hannah:

When I read your words
blood rushes over my face.

Today,
when sirens slashed up Baghdad's sky
I heard you wince and toss.

Do not snore.

We, Americans

were
made
the day
after
nine eleven.

Sweetest,

The lily
blossoming
by
these
red
streams
is
for
you.

Bill Dearest

My breath
is yours
your voice
ours
as we write
our
hearts and souls
dreaming,
feeling,
thinking,
laughing,
giggling
playing.

Your laughter
gurgles from a brook within me.

Drink,
it's pure.

Dearest H:

…Your breath
is mine,
your ink
ours
when we
whisper warm words
to each other,
staring
momentously
at the
disappearing
moon.

As tinkles
from
your spring
adorn me,
my
smile
t
r
i
c
k
l
e
s

i
n
t
o
your
heart.

Listen.

Honey:

Have the flowerbeds been fed?
Are the daisies drinking
from
the
fountain of purity?

Did the aroma
of Espresso
flow
across your bedside
into
the green pastures
beside the lagoon?

Did the phone
wake you up
to another day
of
s
c
r
e
e
c
h
i
n
g

wheels and
sunny
skies?

Did you
soak your

shrine
in
aromatic waters,
halting
to study
your kneecap,
pink toenails,
divine fortress?
Pinkie

Your smile,
fresh
like morning coffee
melts
into my studious stare.

My cucumber
timed to rhyme
with your shrine
could bear fruits
for
eternity.

When I trash my BDU,
you
and
I
could
f
l
y

a
   w
a
   y
to heaven.

Commander Yitzhak

Dressed in my pre-nuptial pink lingerie
with candle lights glowing incessantly,
I stare at the bathroom suit in your wardrobe.

But the hoarse broadcaster says
the battlefield
looms
with corpses of strangers
and familiar ones
lying everywhere,
and
POWs
hurled away
in handcuffs.

That hanger
which held firm
your spacesuit
has not moved.

Commander
Yitzhak,

Come home
to me.

Sweet Pea

Ten thousand feet
below me
are millions of clouds,
lean metallic lanes
sandwiched by square green patches,
undulating hills,
and tiny clustered houses.

But it's not
the Himalayas.

Like veins on a human skeleton
broad and thin lanes
cross each other over the land.
Vehicles
crawl along the lanes
like fleets
of ants.

We zoom low
with busy binoculars.
Still,
I see no one.

Only white clouds
of untold sizes and shapes
and shadows strung against
the water's mighty broad belly
seem to halt eternally.

Once in a while,
something lazily floats
under the clear sky
keeping
my spinning head busy.

continued

The men here are all in green coats
and heavy boots,
and any minute now
these seats will be empty.
My parachute and boots will kiss another foreign soil.

If I never write to you again,
Don't hold an umbrella over your head
and jump from a roof.
My Dearest Hannah:

The B52 bombers
and Tomahawks
are like hawks
poised to
snatch chicks
from Mother Hen.

Did the Wright Brothers
create those birds
to reach God
faster than kites?

Did they
make a recipe
for death?

Why do these hawks
devour
and
disperse us?

The high-cheeked Mulatto nodded
and raised the battery microphone
to his lips:

"The museum
will close in fifteen minutes."

Parents
and their children
shuffled
out
mumbling .

Afterthought

I stared at the B-15
d
   a
     n
gling
from the rooftop
and thought:
"You have led BDUs to creeks
 mountains and deserts.
You burned down nature,
whisked comrades back to safe lands
under enemy fire.

Like a kingfisher
perched on a low tree
by the fish pond,
you
spot
moving objects
through
a tiny hole.

Fire.

Chechnya

As the sun rises,
a Chechnya girl
with blue eyes,
bruised cheek
and hand grenade,
plods
to the convenience store
next door,
stepping
on sharp snow mounds
with naked feet.

The store
bursts
into
flames.

Busy Day

Our chopper
gnawed through the forest,
dropping bombs
like hail stones.

Yusuf and the gang
screamed
and dispersed
as huge balls of fire
sprouted like
goose pimples.

Shrubs
and ghost
cars burned to ashes,
and orchids
spiraled down to join them

Little naked boys
ran
toward their mud-thatched huts,
mucus-nosed children
cried
and
mothers
clutched the earth,

dying.

Men in Jungle BDUs

Men in jungle BDUs
lodged in desert-colored F-15s,
drop leaflets
that
announce freedom

For the countless boys
and girls
with naked torsos,
 freedom brings no wings
to whisk them
to factories
that printed the leaflets.

They read them
with intense desire,
dance joyfully
around gaping grounds
and fuselage
until
more
leaflets
arrive.

While waiting for orders
these men
play gulf
with
bullets,
and comrades
on cannons
cheer
and high-five

continued

when one
hits
the hole.

I can't wait
to meet them
here.

Darling:

So it is
that this lingering soul
will nest on your neck,
rolling ever so close to bliss
so far adrift the carpeted hall
stuffed
with computer wire curtains--
the other sea
I've lived in.

Is it
that someday,
maybe someday,
amid the green,
we will roll and moan
b
e
n
e
a
t
h
your
warm
wet
words?

Ah,
sweet
peace!

Fantôme

It shivers in the cold,
looking around with eyes cold like a gun
for a smile—the chick with no mom.

It plods upon the wet tarmac
throwing furtive glances around
stretching its neck to hear
the familiar voice of matrimony.

Then
it retreats to the veranda
waiting,
shivering,
clucking,
staring,
peering into hedges
to know
if they
are playing
hide-and-go seek.

Inside the purple heart,
la belle dame
aux cheveux longues
avec
la jupe bleue,
et
la sourire merveilleuse
lui dit
en chuchotant,
gekommen!

Zij ligt stil.

Bill

Your presence
is the place
between ink and space.

I explore tracks of time,
stretching my arms
to engulf
dissolving images of you
in the carpeted hallway
and
January seaside.

Facing a heap
of unfinished phrases,
I explore your tracks
to find a text for my heart.

Afghanistan resurging
Hawaii?

Hawaiian Dancer

Do my words rain all over you,
stroking your soul
like a sea leaf
on a nipple?

The chisel,
map,
stone,
space,
wintry cold
caressing my space
is
your presence.

Sweet Hannah

I have come
to mark the atlas of your body
with this tongue.

Driven by a symphony of silence
your voice tells
me
stories
of mermaids and saints
sailing across white seas;
of stars falling and rising;
of jaguars and pintos
coming home for dinner.

Like
a transcontinental passenger
sojourning
in Malaysia,
I wait
to touch you.

I

I,
flea,
live
between silence
and solace
from which
whispers were born,
voiceless,
delirious.

Between tongue
and body,
something comes alive.

Something with a soul,
something to celebrate-
a song.

Sweetheart

My boots are drenched with rain.
Mud has incubated in the other pair.

Like the voiceless cricket
evicted from its hole,
I watch in blazing serenity,
the sun rise and fall.

I see the canopy
s
l
o
w
l
y
shift to next shrub
and then the next.

Butterflies marry the buds
and
divorce them
the next moment.

Like army recruits dropped
on enemy turf,
bees drone about,
unsure
when to cease.

What time is it
in
Colorado?

Time?

When the phone rings,
I whisper a prayer for you.

An unkempt thicket
shivering against the wind.

Tall bush
with a squirrel nest
curved
like a pear.

A storm
beckoning me to listen.

A water hydrant.
A burning heart.
Chills.

Ring,
Ring.

"That was my neighbor checking on me again."

Bill, Guess What

When I heard the bang,
I jumped up from my computer
and rushed towards the TV screen.
Smoke rapidly filled up my room.

I touched my face to wipe sweat,
screamed,
ran outside with a broken arm,
holding my head in my hands,,
searching for human beings.

Bang!
Bang!
Bang!

Sirens.

Flames.

Rooftops exploded.
My neighbors
and strangers
ran about
like cows on a
rampage.

Bang!
We ducked
as blood clusters
formed and streamed
down
footpaths
and
streets.

The Bar

In the bar,
I met a beauty queen
with
long
dark
hair.

Her darting pupils
w
i
g
g
l
e
d
through my BDU,
halting on my
dancing pants.

"Would you be mine
after the war?"
I begged.

She gasped.

Dingy 24 Hours

The soul is midnight.
Dawn breathes Bach and Beethoven.

Morning meets
Streisand at Kennedy Center,
with
Deion
listening.

At lunch,
BB King
and bluegrass
crack open
sounds
of solemn
Wynonas.

Evening returns with
Santana,
Dixie Chicks,
Salsa,
and Britney.

Into my bed
creeps
a symphony of silent memory.

Without my inner guitar,
I can play
25 hours per day.

continued

But why did they
allow
AK47s
and blood
to splatter on the
crescendo?

Had they
ever seen
a child
dancing
with wolves?

The Garden

Have all gardens dried up
from Alaska to the Miami,
leaving the daffodils,
daisies and cherries
to wither
in the bright eyes of spring?

Have your words,
which flowed from the fountain of care
and
landed in the brook of wintered hearts,
jilted time?

What can stop the Battalion from wafting
through carpeted hallways,
spreading harsh verbs at reclining families?

A hotter look
quick intercourse
could breed democratic offspring
someday.

maybe
not.

For Countless Hours

I read your words.
Like the grumpy grandmother in a private ward,
I mime you.

When other patients snore,
I see you
in a dust-littered
desert BDU,
lying among sand dunes
with a machine
gun on your lap,
flies feasting
on your
blood-dressed
face.

The Night in Me

With the night
I stand still,
watching
the river
scuttle
around
the forest floor
unaware of where it's going.

I have a hunch
that when exhausted,
it'll grieve and wait
for my next command.

Stranger

So
distance
makes the heart wither?
Grow heavier,
stranger,
or
dry out?

If not
why do
butterflies
float around my heart,
whenever
I think of
you?

Listen

I perspire,
dreaming
your breath
would
merge
with
mine
tonight.

The Lonely Boy

Green helicopters floated through skies,
dropping balls of death
on camps
and camping grounds
until all
became still.

A Cambodian boy
emerged from a hole
under the mountain
where he had
camped
all
week
and ran to
his ancestral home.

The huts
were a rubble
of dried ghostlike sticks,
smoked clay,
skulls,
and teeth.

When dusk came,
he crawled
down
into the hole
and waited.

Question

Have the rivers dried up
from Alaska to Madagascar,
leaving the daffodils and cherries
to wither
under the bright eyes of spring?

Do your words
flow from the fountain of care
and land in the brook of a wintered heart?

Are they cloaked with desires of me,
or pages
full of empty
promises?

The Konga Player

When you
play the konga,
use my name,
for
Texans
and
hillbillies
only sing blue grass and country;
and multilingual politicians
who've never met me,
can only announce
my
valiance
from
waning microphones
and
colorful tv monitors.

Scene II:

Hannah's Time Alone

Memory Lane 1

Yellow leaves
float around my yard
in search of heat.

Some dare to cross the street
where Mr. Quiet's red Chevy
stands.

My neighbor,
clad in aging wool
and blistered brown gloves,
wipes his nose,
as he sweeps into a sea of heaps,
lifeless grass tufts
and
broken twigs.

Cracked cakes of cold water
smeared
across a tiny pavement
near the barbed wired fence
abruptly halt by the little house
centered in the back lawn.

Florida chairs
surrounding
a droopy canopy
wait for company and
the wet wooden balcony,
as their faithful guardian
with crossed brown arms,
looks on.

The fireplace
is loud and warm.

Thick coats
gathered in a semi-circle
drink rum and tea,
waiting for
the little white gods
to postpone indefinitely
their son's trip to
Baghdad.

Lane 2

The bird far away,
asked bread nearby,
if she could rise earlier
and
snatch it from
the pangs
of darting
ones.

But the bread
said,
"Wait until the cherries
blossom here."

The faithful bird
obeyed.

Lane 3

How could
the bird
so far away,
rise
slightly
earlier
to
snatch
a
piece
of
bread
that
was
unavailable?

Good Morning, America

A Caucasian belle
breast-feeds her infant
 with one eye
pinned against the TV screen.

Guns poised to bite,
dust whirling,
helmets crouched
against smoke-filled walls,
  eyes staring at God,
gashed bowels,
hoofs hurrying through homes
with gaping roofs.
Blue smoke lingering in the air.

Darkness.

Puff.
Puff.

Silence.

Tom's Creed

Tom loved children.
A twenty-one year old wife
survives him.

His son
is only three months old.
Our thoughts and prayers
are with the family.

Next clip.

I
Tremble,
Sob,
collapse
to the
brown-carpeted floor,

weeping
like a willow.

The Lawn Mower

In this garage
I find friends I
have used
for five decades
piously wait for me--
hammer reddened with rust,
screwdriver driven into countless
plywood and doorposts,
chisel
screwing rusty nails
into decomposing timber
and fastening screws in loose rough holes,
tenor saw biting planks ribs,
leaving below
little hills of sawdust
for my
naked eye.

Grabbing
the stubborn tape measure,
I measure wood
with the carpenter's
eye for perfection;

When I ask him to run,
John Deere,
with his keen unsmiling teeth,
sharply severs
the necks of tall grass
that slump
upon each other,
leaving for the eye, a sea
of headless grass.

Of all friends I have used,
the lawn mower
threatens time and age
the most.

Walt Disney

America
and
Paramount pictures
have
merged into
a cacophony
of still
pictures.

In Rio
they call it life
because it
darts across space
and time,
speaking in tongues,
conjuring mammals
to
run
for president,
playing Moses
within
iridescent shrouds
and
a hidden
microphone.

Hannah Meets the Designer

I want
to send
a suit
to
my
husband.

"You need him on your pillow,"
he replies
and
wraps it in a silver bag
and
hands it to me.

Postcards of War

During war,
postcards
are
more beautiful
than clothes.

Send them
to your husband.

Celebrate
your
birthday.

Soldier

Your atlas
harbors
hungry nations.
A chest full of roses.

A colored butterfly
from
a barren land
has landed
on your cheek.

Let your blue eyes
close.

Hear
the night
flutter around
you.

Your body
a musical
statue,
naked.

Whisper
any
word.

Father's Day

A father is
a guide,
a pen,
paper,
name.

A father is
the good spirit
running through me,
urging me
to stand and
keep running
when
I fall.

A father is
the stern voice
I hear
when I falter.

A father is
the carpenter,
the lawyer,
the farmer.

A father is
the hummer humming
through the streets of life
in search of life's fruits
to nourish my mind.

A father is
the door of happiness that opens
when the other one has closed.

Aren't there moments
when you miss your father
so much you just want
to lift him from the wreckage in
your dreams and hug him?
Of those many million hours
you've invested in me,
here's one glowing gift for you.
Happy Father's Day.

Independence Day

Here
birds sing for silent souls
and perch upon engraved words.

This place paved
with graveled paths,
aligned tombs
tall and short
with stars and stripes
pinned next to each tomb.

The flags flutter
as gentle winds breeze by
and head
toward
the pines
and whipping willows
near the pond
until
darkness
arrives.

I leave
wondering whether
I betrayed them
by
not calling
my senator
to vote
against the war.

A Glimpse of Death Walking

Who are those thin-necked turbans
with soiled toe-deep garments
sauntering
abreast a tired
grey hill,
with blistered AK-47s,
wounded missiles,
and hand grenades
strapped
to their shoulders?

Are they bringers of peace
in Afghanistan,
forsaken with land mines?

Veteran

(The poet was invited to prepare and read a poem on Veterans Day, 2005, at the Camden Court House, North Carolina. The Boy scouts, Knights of Columbus Squad and Second World War Veterans were in attendance It follows.)

You marched
to Normandy, Hiroshima, Nagasaki, Korea,
Vietnam, and to
he Gulf.
Two million of you were dispatched on June 17, 1917.
You came to Camden.
You joined arms with comrades from across the oceans,
and spoke of freedom.

Lying on a bunker
you wrote sweet letters to your children.
You married her and returned to fire.

You gulped sleepless nights under hot desert soil.
You
plodded through deep dismal swamps
and thick dark forests
dodging booby traps,
with eyes fixed on death.

You read Lincoln, Wilson, Truman, Roosevelt, Nixon, Washington,
Bush.
You joked and laughed with General MacArthur.

The USS Battleship,
tank and Air Force One,
fluttering with Red, White and Blue stars,
took you to lands far and unfamed.

You returned with a stained flag.

Graves, Van Dyke, Foster, Herbert, Owen,
and those Americans
adorn you today.

Infantry
Brigade
Platoon
Battalion

Soldier!
Give Him your hand.
America

Should I hail 1812-1815 heroes
or the Creeks?

Should I salute troops who toiled
and bled
struck and ducked enemy fire
in Georgia,
Hiroshima,
Normandie,
Vietnam,
Kuwait,

Baghdad?

I salute America.
I salute Lincoln,
Douglass,
and
Bethune Cookman
who
sang my name
when I was born?

I toast
Samuel Adams,
Paul Revere, and
Jefferson.

I
dump
Oklahoma anti heroes
and
Sept. 11 blood drinkers.

I
salute
Him
because He
looks after His sheep
from dusk to dawn.

From Love to Freedom?

From your infancy,
 you learned about liberty's light
from the old book.
You savored it on the Mayflower
on swaying boats
and dark seas.

You wafted amidst rough seas
as we sang
cried
and
prayed.

We fed your industry
with raw food harvested from my ribs.

When you liberated mankind
from the pangs of dictators,
Our grandsons and
siblings offered you their homes
and hearts for your refuge.

Together
we claimed the mindless ones
—for freedom.

You led us here
fed us
when they had declared us clinically dead.
You healed our hurt
with healthy laws.
You clothed us with choices,
love.
liberty,
and the freedom to shout.

You taught us to live with dignity,
to serve freedom

Your zest for humanity zooms through rough turf with blessed force.
Your moon blows out a purple star.
You sing the Star Spangled Banner with different voices.

This poem was prepared to be read Veterans Day, Nov. 2003 at the
Camden Court House
Soldier

You returned hoarse.

Disarm!

Scene III:

Bill's Time Alone

My Bedroom

When I signed my name,
no one told me
I'd share my bed
with frogs and snakes
and wall geckoes
in swamps taller than Everest.

Success,
Captain Tall preached,
is sweetest
when you
spill bullets
at racing insurgents.

Bowser,
Mark ,
and Takahara
ducked and ran.

But look to my right.
Their t-shirts
and lovers' photos
lie on the wet mattress
and lonely bunk bed,
waiting
forever
for their return.

A Voice Overseas

Burning with wrath,
my heart swells
when white-robed,
rose-lipped ladies
are left
to die in fields
where light-footed lads live.

The footpaths
of escaping civilians
are
too broad
for deer's leaping.
Goats and chickens
 too scared
to roam
as countless voices
of AK-47s
rivet
the wilderness.

The infant's cry
for food
is drowning.

The Forgotten Name

This gun,
like a crooked song,
lies in my sweating hands
waiting for a stir in the thicket.

At day,
my fingers play on the trigger
like a frenetic singer
in a crowded opera hall.

For five months
this
wrinkling 34-year old body
clad in a soaked BDU,
boots cloaked
with red mud-cakes
sang "America the Beautiful,"
hrough
deep dismal swamps.

Soldier's Wish

If my wife
were here
she would
wash my garments,
buy me coats
and shoes,
dress our bed
with cotton pillows,
cook infinitely,
and massage me.

There are
no malls here
and
no personal links.

Only
priceless
treasures
and
eternally
happy hearts.

Oftentimes

I stare at a B52 bomber
p
e
e
l
i
n
g
the landscape,
and I grow fearful of it.
A tiny white ghost within
this dark room
stares at me
with milky eyeballs.

Always true to time and man,
it speaks to me in Hebrew:
"They shall not raise the sword against another
nor shall they train for war again."

I genuflect and whisper to him:
"They swing their swords marching into Jerusalem,
stripping life in Gaza."

But why
has this linguistic ecstasy
been persuaded
by abjection?

Why
does Captain Lucifer
speak all languages?

Is Pope John Paul II
still

on his knees
in the Vatican
with hands
clutched to the cross?

Do priests
and bishops
still say Mass
in Latin?

The Hallucinatory Truth

My life that started with a panegyric
 at thirty-five,
has
r
o
l
l
e
d
into the oil refinery
with bumps and
twists so c r o o k e d,
language
cannot
mold it.

At twenty-one
the surgeon stitched my unfinished words,
and
stuffed my bowels
with glittering pictures of heaven.

Then
he bid me,
"Go back to life,
tell him you can."

I consulted life daily.

One morning
I heard:
"Your sorrows are joy unmasked.
Joy is stronger than sorrow."

I bumped into a jazzy car.
I saw a man
smiling
softly.

Swathed in large garments
that glittered
like a Christmas tree, he said,
"Come.
Come away with me."

The Infantry's Childhood Days

In those days,
Jaguars
clad in tawny black rosettes
and dunlop jackets
dashed across fields
in search of game.
Their bright eyes and teeth
smiling
at the unwitting squirrel
they
stopped for lunch.

The jaguar stood in the middle of the road
like king of the jungle,
daring the racing cougar
to hit him.

His legs
squeaking
for an oily massage,
his fur
whipped
by thunderstorms and summer suns,
his feet
having smashed
every leaf in the jungle,
he crawled
along the tarmac

I wonder what he'll
do
when the wildcat,
Bronco,

continued

panther
and
bobcat
come back.

Building My Heart

Like a passing wind
it faded.

I looked up
hoping it would ring again.
Having placed my heart
on your cheek,
I raised
your blue eyelids
to catch your smile.

Smile?
Unfinished roof.
These planks,
cement,
nails,
marble,
and the carpenter
expect light
from this dark hole
of bottomless bliss.

How infectious the war
that brought him here.

A Pre-War Briefing

My dear boy scouts,
Did you know
that your letters never reached us?
Did you know
that the mailman on a camel back
made a bonfire with them
and went home by day?

Which ones were addressed
to Captain Idriss Miskina?
Private Bantu,
and
Second Lieutenant Bahrain?

Who snapped the toy pistol
from my son's hand
during Compton Lane parade
and
brandished red, white and blue flags?

Who whispered
romantic tunes
in Bessie's right ear,
and whisked her away
when Jake Plumber's float
crashed into the grandstand?

Who saw her putting back lipstick?
Who knows
when she returned
to the parade?

I will not return enemy fire
today!

Prom Night

The band that played till dusk,
banged deep into my soul,
and dug out pictures
of me conducting,
as our award-winning
Currituck High School Band
marched
in glory
at half time.

You waved that flag,
yelling
like a witch
possessed by hungry demons.

Do you remember?
Or
am I
seventeen
again

Bloodshed

Mountains of human flesh sleep eternally
in this cold dark room.

Some do not know if their sibling may visit.
Some do not know where their souls have gone.

But
I have spotted some
in ragged black twills
lingering
around abandoned battlefields,
grabbing grenades
with feeble hands,
aiming at their perennial enemy
—peace.

They cry,
wail,
stutter

and
b
l
e
e
d
profusely.

Mr. Democrat

Why did you
not
tell me
you
would
pave
my
streets
with
mire
when
you
brought scud missiles
and
dethroned
the Persian empire?

On Break

Pain lingers
in this theater
as we
gulp qwacha.

Some kiss gin tumblers,
dance rock-n-roll
with Vietnamese belles,
and
sleep
with
unmasked Basra wives
until
dawn,

while
we
laugh, and
\poke fun
at each other
before
we
wear
the mask,

pull
triggers,

fire.

Veteran Fighter

Brandishing a menacing gaze,
a pistol aimed at turbans,
we plod along hot sand mounds
to
the
next
village.

We
peer into the hole
with a strained eye,
fingers trembling
to pull the trigger again.

The sky turns
crimson,
beckoning a silent cry
for my grandchildren
and neighbor's siblings
dancing on the trampoline.

Shivers rock me,
for grief
is no choice
for a man
whose morning beverage
was
blood.

Memorial Day,
July Fourth,
9/11.

Do
not
return!

After the Battle

Last night's storm
that humbled a baobab
and assembled little lakes
ten miles apart
is gone.

Velvet dreams
and
boot prints reign
here.

Your children
see
flower gardens,
sniff
clean air,
eat
sumptuous dinners,
play
scrimmage football, and
chat with neighbors
living across the bridge.

Here
my head
is loaded
with
cartridges.

My gardens
watered with
fresh human
blood.

A Street in Mecca

After fifteen months
nobody knows this place.

Only anguish,
ashes,
and
acronyms
halt
for peace.

From afar
the cackle
of a tambourine,
cacophony
of Nakata's violin,
and
mad strokes
of Ibrahim's drum
rock my soul
as
I
stroll
and
trudge
on skeletons
from other regions.

I must not
blast
their drums.

I didn't
create them.

The Polished AK-47

In a warm night like this,
with the moon half full
and a cool breeze
whispering through these huge,
dark trees,
my AK-47
stays beside me
poised to kill.

My mind sees
Jill,
Jake,
Becky
and
Ashley
shooting basketball,
playing poker,
tickling each other,
hugging,
winning.

I wait for orders
to shoot
invisible balls
and win fields
for my country.

Win
what?

Looking for Virgin Island

This Woodland Camouflage has been
glued to my body
for ten weeks.

My body
speaks toxic odors.
My fierce helmet
always ready to go.

My bald head
stocks
rivers
of
sweat.

This morning,
Captain Hamburger
has told us a shipment
of new Tiger Stripes
arrives next week.

Next month,
we see
the desert camouflage.

We will
wear them,
salute him
and
die.

continued

But
we have been dying
since
being
deployed
here.

Scene IV:

Israeli-Palestinian Olympics

Students at War

Studying the Kabala
is not like
reading a magazine
full of iron-faced generals
and
lieutenants
clad in thick black suits.

It is
not
for medievalists
nor for
the semi-comatose.

It is a training manual
for real power,
true humanity,
fulfillment.

It
nourishes the spirit.

The new map in progress
nourishes
greed.

The Community of Nations

Teargas,
stun guns,
grenades
and
stones flying.

Fluttering fags on tankers.

Gaza.
Ramallah.

A throng
marching
to the graveyard
with the fallen soul
of
another teenage
male.

Is this all
I can offer the world
on
my
60th
anniversary?

The Martyr

u
with walky-talkies
in their mouths
and
ears
scurry
to a bashed car,
sizzling
from a bomb blast.

They
thrust
clenched fists
in mid air
and
march to
the state border
to
escort
death.

An Old Death Threat

Hands lift up a coffin
clothed with
the Star of David
and parade
the streets of Jerusalem
singing Halleluiah.

We will settle!

We will settle
where
they
chant
incessantly
in Arabic.

Bomb Center

They call it Tel Aviv
because natives
chant apologies at sundown,
attend shrines by day
looking for God.

They live
on farms,
not theatres.

They
sing
"thank you very much"
when pain
invades their minds.

The city in
Yankee land
is a pond peopled
with croakers
scrambling
to
hide from gunshots,

It harbors
salmons
that sting croakers
with their fins
searching
for
real estate
for their colony.

Terrorists in Our Backyard

Her back,
languishing on the straw mattress,
 eyes
watching God in a ceiling light,
arms and legs
outstretched,
she
dreams of futons
and Paris towers.

Bruised belly sinking and rising,
tubes and wires connected to her frame
like Delta's global flight map,
she expels huge breath bouts.

As you watch her negotiate death
in this room where light shines all day,
where white aprons,
lab coats and surgical scrubs
incessantly visit cubicles,
firm arms press the chest,
blowing life into the stalled heart,
where were you,
 when she took the grenade to
 the school playground?
Where were you
 when they hurled stones at flying bullets?
Where were you
 when a tourist bus
bound for the scenic West Bank
exploded
and
Prometheus

erased trails
filled with truth?

What did you hear
as life
crept out of their bodies?

The Prayerful Priestly Soldier

You sit
on this
century-old mat
thumbing the Torah,
lisping,
thinking yoga,
conjuring Imams,
the Sabbath.

Rabbis
keep candles,
the infinite
life
glowing.

Double explosions
in Haifa.

We're all numb!

Allah,
have mercy on Khadija.

Military Intelligence

When Scud
read the Koran
he thought he was ready
to fight.

How clever he was
in visualizing winning
in the birthplace of freedom.

Mr. Freedom

Why did you tell me
my children
would worship
Allah
in mosques and streets,
yet that long blonde hair
still plods
my villages,
giving away pamphlets on
the Jewish prophet?

You told me Persian martyrs
were cancer in my bones—
that I could go to Jericho,
sing
with Travis Tritt
and
dance
with Travolta.

You
brought me bags
of wheat
because my fields
wither too soon.

I've seen
your images
of
four-wheeled people
and skyscrapers.

You courted us
for decades.

We bought
your technology,
oiled your roads,
furnished
your homes.

Why
are you
here?

Lebanon in 2006

Rage
cooked with
hypocritical holiness
jams the skies
from
Tehran
to Damascus,
from
Jerusalem
to Ras Bayada.

Flying rockets
land on mountains and homes.

Metallic stars
zoom down
like a hawk stealing a chick,
swiping lives.

Anti-tank platoons
TOWs,
Golani Brigades
arrive firehouse unnumbered.

The 609th Reserve Infantry
c
a
v
e
into familiar turf
gnawing towns.

By dusk
one hundred and thirty buildings
in Haret Hreik
leveled.

Who else was there?

Another fireball
in Tel Aviv!

Didn't rockets
land there last night?
UN Headlines

The world says,
blow
off
the
smoke
from
those
senseless
mouths.

Young Warrior

At seventeen
I matched forward
with them
and
butchered youth
in Kuwait,
prompted
by
lies.

You
decorate me
with metal.

You
give me hickeys
and
ask for a ring

You praise
my butchery.

Pray for my soul!

Blood on the Walls

Back against the hollow wall
arms stretched away;
palms bloodless,
wrists
tied with goat rope,
face
riddled with bullets,
stomach gaping,
mouth and nose
dripping with blood,
torso naked,
breathless.

The brown haired captive
stares
at the open door
defiant,
waiting for life.

The stench
of Arabian sweat
still lingers
in the roofless room.

Scene V:
Desert Storms

Pictures of Fire

At seven,
a plane
dressed in green camouflage
glided across the screen
and touched down
in the Amazonian forest.

Green berets
rushed out
aiming their guns
at a crowded marketplace.

Turbans.

Unshaved chins,
wrangler jeans
charged at them,
unleashing an arsenal
of pebbles.

Our eyelids
disorganized,
we grimaced
as veiled women
in black gowns
wailed,
pointing
to shackles
on their bruised ankles.

To its bottom right,
lying prostrate,

was a long white gown,
its clenched fist,
resting
on sandy ground.

"Fire!"

Anthills in the Desert

The anthills
we built across clear land
are no more.

Only a twig
and a tired leaf
d
r
o
p
to the ground;
and
rodents occasionally
move about,
unconcerned
by my presence.

My partners
d
r
a
g
their bellies
along the scrubby thicket,
aim their ever-smoky gun mouths
at the
enemy camp.

But
no shots were fired
yesterday.

I don't hear
the subdued breathing of a tired soldier.

continued

Have the booby traps
eaten
them
up?

Or
did the Taliban
scurry them to their theatre
in blindfolds?

The Martyr

As Abu Azzam lay on dry grass
dying,
with
fresh blood oozing
from his
right
rib
stung
by a
Yankee bullet,
the distant face of triumph,
agony,
and foreign cameras
adorned the world.

Zarqawi
told
Abu Musab,

"We
must
return
the favor
or
we're nothing!"

A shrill voice
cried from the wire,
"A painful
blow
to the country's
most feared
insurgent group,"

continued

and
retreated
to its shadow.

Bodies
litter
the
streets
of Baghdad!

Weih!, Weih

View in a Theater

Why are those girls
marching
in Bushra Jabar's brigade
under
this broiling morning sun?

Has Khawla Bint al-Awar
disguised to join the fight?

I
will
not
drop
my
arms
to
hug
them.

Yankees
cannot
fight
Muslim
wars!

Day 10

There's only gray sand
and winds
here.

Winds blowing sand,
brown sky falling,
men on horses
galloping toward us
with spears
hoisted in mid air.

God
is
not
here.

Libertarian at Battlefront

Turn off Heavy D and
Stop the engine.

Don't watch the stocks.
Release your cat.
Look through your window.
Planes
are crashing
on rooftops again.

Stop the taxi.
Stop the trains.
Suspend the First Amendment.
Search
every man and woman
here.

Close
the borders.

Listen
to all cell phone
conversations.

Arrest them!

Take
them
to
jail.

Strip
them
naked.

continued

Beat
them
black
and
blue.

Tear up
their
passports.

Sierra Leone

Tornado!

Rich shopper
racing
through
jewelry stores,

Armed juvenile soldiers
crowding paved streets
firing,

gathering goods
saved
for African refugees.

Don't
shoot
the
UN.

My Dearest Sweetheart

Your twinkling eyes,
guitar body,
Verizon Wireless voice
rekindle
the moral immaturity
of
my
amorous
adventures.

Look at the blood
on my eyeballs
scuffed
by rifle shots.

My heart is locked up--
its keys
in a dark place.

What
don't
you
understand?

The Regiment

Under the scorched sun
they kneel
before a soul
whose membranes
are splashed
a
  c
    r
      o
        s
          s
a mud brick wall.

Missiles
vying
for aerial control
roam Baghdad skies.

Flames
claim
Tikrit
in
sixty
minutes.

Lieutenant,
his leg
has moved!

Dead bodies
everywhere.

continued

Tuff!
Tuff!
Tuff!

Smoke
envelopes
the whole place.

The Militia

Do not
remove the last bullet
from this knee.
Let me
eat the mamba's bile
alone
and expire.

Zarqawi
watches him die
as his deputy
spies the skies
for the faintest
signs
of invaders.

The resurgents
retreat to
their caves
and
rocks

for siesta.

Yankee birds
drop
loud bombs
and
run away.

You, America

You told me to take my bags
to the train station
and fly over this land
 to wide arid fields.

You sang my name
on every TV show.

You told me you'd pray
for my safe return.

I guarded desert oil fields
for you.

My feet
sank into
boiling sand
as the typhoon
swooped
t
h
r
o
u
g
h
our camp
blowing
every piece
of anguish
into our eyes.

When
will
I
return
home?

Tell me now!

Epitaph

If we
return home,
will McDonalds
stay open?

Will my pastor
clean the blotches
from my eyes?

Will he
slam
the chapel door
and order me
to leave?

Will I become
Forbes' neighbor in Madagascar
and die with a martyr?

Will the inscription
on my tomb read:
"Here lies the man who bombed innocent children
and ate a lamb's heart at a Campaign dinner party?"

Will it read:
"Here
lies the man
who gave his country everything
he didn't have,
and they left
when he was named
Guest of Honor
at the veteran's parade?"

"Here lies the man who loved his

his sweetheart so much
he expired without her saliva on his lips?"

"Here lies the man
who loved his country so much he's grateful
they don't visit his graveyard?

Let me try this,
"Here lies the soldier
who aspired to trump up
his life but
his leg was left
to rot in a field
stranger than his town."

Which statement
will appear
on my tomb?

A Soldier's Mother

These boots
they left in this house,
resemble those of
the living dead.

Other boots stay at borders,
dismantled
by philanthropists,
corporate executives,
cell phones.

Some
who speak German,
Yiddish,
Portuguese,
Swahili,
Japanese,
English,
have lived there
since 1945.

They
play football
with their
grandchildren
while their ancestors
wait
for orders
to
return home.

Actual News

A loud explosion
The train
grinds to a
s
c
r
e
e
c
h
i
n
g
halt.

Screams.
Darkness.
Stampede.

Hammers
bang on windows.
Sirens.
Radios.

Fifty dead!

Hundreds of casualties
hauled on stretchers
across
business district
into bloated hospitals

continued

Who
killed
London
that July morning?

A Patriot's Creed

Have I lost my
patriotic longings
by singing
the praises
of a great soldier?

Has he
gained my trust
in knowing
I care
about his wife,
about toddlers
he
left
behind
to protect
the lands of
the Hittites?

He told me
though some
salute
the
flag
and
take the oath,
they're stiff
with fear.

Their feet
suffocate
in boots
scuffed

continued

with sand
and
wear.

He
mumbled
and
whispered,

"I wanted
to stay home."

The Lebanese Palestinian

The winds of Fall
blowing across
Israel
and
Syria
collect leaves
abandoned by
recent
memories
of
blood
baths.

Lebanese children
trudge back
home
to pick up
house keys
dropped
by
war.

Baghdad at Noon

When
I
turn on my binocular,
a man on a camel
loaded
with bags
of grenades
plods across
the desert
in search of
Yankee berets.

I
spot a turban
with a machine gun
strapped to his
shoulder.

He
furtively glances
at the skies.

When a bomb
lands
in the
marketplace,
he
jerks up his
AK-47;
fires
ten rounds,
and

tilts his head
like
a
squirrel.

Victory Lap

They
drive
through the streets
of Baghdad,
New York,
Washington
tooting horns,
waving flags,
and
white scarves
for the home team.

Children
stay up late
banging tin cans.

Immigrants,
legal and forged,
drive
by Power Avenue
honking
and
waving
multicolored flags,
singing
in two hundred languages,
some in gibberish,

"Viva Freedom!"

But
no one has seen
these
empty beer cans
and whisky bottles

in
my
bedroom
beckoning
me
to
another
war.

Baghdad Hospital

Debris.
Dust everywhere;
artillery
flying helter-skelter;
men in camouflage
coughing,
racing madly for shelter.

Police car lights
flashing profusely,
the ambulance
rushing toward
the Tamahawk,
blood oozing
through
the battered camouflage.

Doctors calling doctors.
Nurses running into bloody rooms
in face masks,
with blunt scissors

The latest amputee
nearby
gazes at the door
to catch a glimpse
of his new roommate,
before dying.

On the wooden bed,
they drop another BDU,
tear his dusty garments,
and work in frenzied motion
on his
blood-bleached chest.

He breathes faster,
pants,
his sun-tanned face
languishing in terror.

The machine above his bed
chants on like a time bomb
waiting to be silenced.

A Young Soldier's Tears

Computerized prosthetics;
man walking on iron legs,
shops waiting,
prom nights sour,
dates lost.

Anger recovered.
Purple heart
s
p
r
e
a
d
across my bed;
white aprons
sneering,
white robes
taking turns
holding my wrist,
counting my pulse—
hours
left
on
my
life.

A Mother's Question

They say war
is no longer
declared,
only continued.

Just because
life changes
Doesn't mean
it must stop.

Is this
another media buzz?
A politician
playing for votes?

Is Parkinson's
better than a
young
soldier
on
crutches?

War Songs

My head purrs like a war song,
chanted with jazzy madness.

But when the bugle prompts,
we jump down from our bunk beds,
pull up our mud-caked trousers
and assemble under the tent
—our living room,
for last minute mappings
and strategy.

With brave hearts
we sing and march forward.

Left,
right,
left,
right,
we march,
swinging one arm
with our gun butts in our palm.

Gun mouths on our shoulders
chests arched forward,
eyes fixed at space,
we march onward,
toward death.

Fearing not the sight of bullets
buried in our comrades' foreheads,
we march for country,
for a name.

We march for the flag.
Red

White
Blue.

Green white green.
Yellow red white.
Purple.

We march
for purple hearts.

The Marching Band

This morning,
we left a dozen.
None dismayed.

Onward
we marched.

We marched
down the valley of death,
some on horseback,
others on tankers,
by air,
in ships.

We galloped
though we knew
some had blundered.

Away
we galloped,
while they
threw poisoned spears at us,
swearing by Allah:

"This is our land,
Draculas!"

"Allah strike you dead!"
they yelled,
firing ten, twenty rounds at once.

"Evil empire
satanic rifles,
return to your country!"

"We will not be conquered!"
some announced
approaching
our firing frame.

"Engage!"

Missiles fled and exploded on rough turf.
Large balls of fire sprouted across the desert.

Day 367

At dawn,
machine guns
sang
endlessly
near
our tent.

Our platoon
fed their rifles
and
fired countless rounds
at turbaned men
racing
toward them
on wild horses,
carrying
machine-guns.

Cease fire!

I paused
like a rabbit
to listen
to
sporadic
shooting.

In front me
around me
lay comrades
with eyes
staring at me

forever.

Shattered legs

Shattered legs,
gaping holes on chests,
blood bathed machine guns,
hands clutched to rifles.

Fly infested eyes staring at the sky.
Bodies
l
y
i
n
g
prostrate
next
to each other,
waiting
to be rested with dignity.
Hearts
begging for mercy.

Is this Kabul,
Tel Aviv
or the America
I drink?

When can our glory
fade
or return?

When will
those wild freedom claims
we have made
arrive in
Afghanistan?

continued

When
will we
appease
the world
after
decorating
our
fallen
soldier?

Senseless Acts of War

Long,
steel guns,
from war ships
that bear red white and blue
pointing at green pastures
across oceans
and seas.

White blouses
sitting in boats singing war songs.

Ships sailing
toward flags ashore I can't read.

Tankers rolling across the Sahara
with hidden helmets inside
poised like Robbin Hoods at night.

Neat,
polished
machine guns.

Tan faces,
sealed mouths
clad in camouflage suits
and knee-deep boots
with machine guns
glancing through the thickets
below.

Black balls
dropping from helicopters,
striking fire,
loosening turf.

Abandoned naked children
crying.

Parents half-clothed.
Wild dogs barking nonstop.
Cats,
goats
and horses
running wildly.

Battlefront

Blue smoke.

Cumulus skies.

Rumbles.

Pang! Pang!
on and on,
deafening ears.

Fire mountains
sprouting everywhere.

Bodies with pointed guns
collapsing
like chopped trunks.

Infants,
boys,
girls,
mothers,
grandparents
falling around
like flies sprayed with Roach Bomb.

Body parts
scattered.

Fat flies
still feasting
on holes
beneath
bullet-torn BDUs.

Nurses
in mud-thatched huts,
with blocked nostrils
dipping wet sponges
into bloody
gaping holes.

Peace is
Still
on vacation!

Animals

Domestic animals
are hovering around these huts
alone.

Breathless bodies
abandoned
in the fields.
Their eyes
begging for
one
more
chance
to live.

Villagers
camped in a secret shelter.

Soldiers with fingers on the trigger,
patrol the village outskirts.

Helicopters droning,
wounded men on hand-held stretchers
groaning.

Stretchers
rushing away from the helicopter,
women in white gowns
wearing red cross hats
washing fresh wounds in windy tents.

Half the insurgents
are rushing back to their cave,
blowing out smoke from their guns.
Frogs croaking.
Lanterns shadowed by bamboo fences.

Soldiers loading cartridges,
tankers refueling,
Captain Death
debriefing the last of his men.

Fireballs rising a mile away.
Flames roasting a mosque.
Barns burning.

The Situation Room

Two months,
four years gone.
The servants
ask
the Lieutenant:

"What time is this?
Where are we now?
When will we return home?"

Another missile
lands
near the tent.

Scene VI:

World Games

Angola

A ruinous
27-year civil
war
killed
one million people,
destroyed
your
infrastructure,
leaving you
at the basement
of the south end.

Today,
your children
cry victory
as you march
to World Cup
Germany
hugging
Jornal de Angola
and Eduardo dos Santos.

Viva
Angola?

Dalfour Again

Brown earth patches
interspersed
with stunted trees
dotted
across the wilderness

Dusty tracks,
gray roof tops ,
branches
of cracked brooks,
tributaries,
helicopters
peopled
with guns,
spears,
arrows
aiming
at dying voices.

Malinke.
Hutu.

Darfour.

Tutsi children
sing
dirges about farms
filled with dead bodies.

Child soldiers
comb the wilderness
searching
for family teeth
and elephant tusks
they

can hide
from
massacre
experts.

Have nations united
against
those?

Vietnam Reborn

This prima donna
with hips
full of dynamite
like a mud-clotted macho
in Vietnam
and desert storm manager
studied militia might
in
Harvard's grand canyon.

She parades
across your screen
confessing
her plot with
her dead husband,
vowing
to return
to the West Bank
dead.

When Zarqawi falls,
she will
explode
in a mall
near you.

Tell me,
will you
leave home
without it?

An Abandoned Bunker

Your hand
is theirs;
your keys,
ours.

When we visit
all nations
on bunkers,
cruising by trucks
engulfed in fuselage,
stay alert.

We will halt for fuel
at stations
manned by ostrich feathers.
Broad turbans,
crying masks,
ostrich feathers,
satin birds
and
red faces
with diminished smiles.

When we
find rivers
flooding with global goods
we will redirect the
flood toward
the western hemisphere,
wrecking fresh plants
in emerging farms.

continued

There,
we will
enlist lads
raised
to sing their native songs
and
hear their national anthems.

Leave
your
children
in Europe.

Soldier's Journey

Night's face
unparsed
by
heat.

Light
i
n
v
a
d
e
s
dawn,
weeping.

My tanning
face
shines
with
last week's
sweat.

Yours
was tanned
from birth.

Trudge on,
soldier.

The Global Village

Patel

Manglik,

Kaiser,

Jeffers,

Rahim,

Majinda,

Jorge,

Wang Yu.

United
to
kill?

Neighbor Remembers

Where are the heroes
of the fifth battalion?
Where's the rough neck,
red eye,
stolid face?

They are lying still
in the valley.

One fell on his shotgun.
One was burned by friendly fire.
One collapsed on a bridge.
One died with a cloth strapped to his mouth.
One drowned in the waterfall.
All are lying still in the valley.

Where are their sweetened hearts?
Where're the tender love birds that moan at night?
They are lying in the valley.

One died writing a letter.
One drowned from thwarted love.
One gave birth to another man's child.
One joined the crusaders in search of a name.
One lost her house keys,
her kids still in school.
One wired love to men in Australia,
Kuala Lumpur.
One bought a net to catch phallic symbols.
All are lying still in the valley.

They brought them dead flags,
folded colored cloths.

continued

Jones,
Tommy,
Lisa,
and Colonel Sharp
who had preached for days
of Iraqi freedom,
and weapons of mass destruction,
are
lying still in the valley
dead.

Public Announcement: A Soldier Speaks of War: First Lecture

I was the first fruit from Camden, North Carolina
to throw myself
at the battleship
that arrived
at our shore.

My
great
grand
son
was the first soldier
to march
through the daunting forests
in Panama.

I watched parrots
and pigeons
build their nests in Vietnam.

I had read
with awe
the wry chants
of Isaac Rosenberg,
Rupert Brooke,
Robert Graves,
and Robert Van Dyke.

I mangled through
the raw words
of 1st Lt. John R. Fox,
Vernon Haywood
Dorie Miller;

continued

and other
Buffalo soldiers,
basked in their glory.

When some
revisited the Harbor
and invoked Hiroshima,
I claimed
German heritage
and spoke proudly
of the Niger.

A Soldier Speaks of War: Second Lecture

Good day,
everyone.

During our 25th wedding anniversary,
I told them
marriage is a soft voice
shouting atop a mountain.

"Wrong again,"
my wife shouted,
"It's the triumph
of experience
over death.

Which one
Didn't you choose?"

My speech today,
is no match
for her wisdom.

To those of you
still thinking
about it,
I say
just don't do it.

When another bullet
whistled past my chest
and peeled a tree trunk nearby,
I wish
I had stayed home
and enlisted in jail.

This granite
is my old friend
the battlefield,
my time.

My spirit
incessantly sings
pro patria muri--
the new anthem
of my life.

True Soldier

Here're my legs
crushed under a tanker?

I sit on a wheel chair by the street corner
with a shabby coat and my star-spangled hat
like smiling Uncle Sam's.

Jingling this rusty mug
like Santa on Boxing Day
I hear boys and women
urging each other,
"Show your Patriotism!
Drop it here!"

I cry
like
those in Vietnam forests.

I cry
like the naked
Vietcong orphan
who
ran wild
in front of cameras
screaming,
terrified
by my monstrous face--
this gun
they had seen
blasting
away their villages.

I blink,
pray,
and
halt my breath
for a moment.

Why
did
we
do
that?

Good Riddance

How can I,
Mr. Erudite preacher,
who summoned the world,
spied on trucks hauling away weapons
across discussed borders,
I
who saw human shadows
and metallic birds
f
    l
  y
    i
       n
  g
safely
across skies into foreign lands
sit here
and watch this children's day care center
go down
in flames,
dismantled by a missile?

I
who dashed verbal swords
at children of Babylon?

How is it that Mr. Erudite,
who saw children's blood
splashing across birthday cakes,
ordered another missile
to blow up a mountain,
disperse grazing cattle,
and lay bare
the bowels

of unarmed women
in the marketplace?

Tell me why I lie here
unnamed
while Dalmer,
the city's beef eater,
has his name engraved
in marble
on his tomb?

Militia Awards

The militia crowned me mayor
When migrant workers were shipped out of town,
because I, retired Lieutenant Broad, had slaughtered,
in drunken rage,
unclothed Africans.

I watched with a wrysmile
Rwandan children starving to death,
And became the Born-again Christian.
And they wanted a man
with courageous vile, wanton smiles and a kind heart,
a hater of the poor and lover of drunkards,
to restore law and order in the city of angels.

And they gave me the town's key,
a gun police wear
to patrol the streets with them.

I pulled it from underneath my rib
and shot Jorge Paez
twice in the head at midnight.

At dawn, a bullet struck Yerima's heart,
I can't pronounce his last name.
But he didn't die.

To hang him was my dream
but hunters
might find him later
and an investigation would find me,
I grunted.

I jumped into my jeep,
winked a cautious warning
at Ted,

continued

Bill
and
Brad
and
drove to my office.

Three terms in office
were enough to fire me
Sixty-two years are enough to kill me.

In Whose Name?

My girlfriend birthed twins.
My mother lost her health
and expired in a nursing home,
with her back against the earth,
her eyes watching God.

And that bloke
whom women named Kennedy,
came along
and stole her heart
and eloped with my babies.

Death emerged
from a raging truck,
and crushed them,
one by one.

And I,
adorned by God's grace,
crouched behind a lantern-lit table beside my iron bed
composed countless letters and poems
for Ashley and Bryant the bloke,
Tammie and Mom.

They moved me
from
Cagliari
to Bonn.

From Germany
to the Mexican border,
to

continued

Panama,
Bosnia,
and
now
Lebanon?

I must
plant my coconut tree in Baghdad today
else they'll have me packing
for
Syria,
Venezuela

I'm not a Damn Yankees

Lucille,
do not weep.
I am not in this box.
The winds of spring,
aroma of green grass
are with me.
There're no cannons
or
smoke or fear here.
No captains or generals.

Muslims,
Jews
and Gentiles I killed
are not clad in war clothes.

We wear
one brand of clothing
and eat together.

Souls from
Nigeria,
Peru,
Mississippi,
Nagasaki,
Sidney,
Auckland,
Normandie,
eat countless
last suppers
together.

continued

Go home.
Save
my
decorated
cap
for Brandon
till
he
turns
eighteen.

Frosty Flakes for Dinner

You see red, white and blue flags fluttering
all over this quiet place,
stretched away with cemented mounds and flowers of all kinds.

You see brown,
black and pink birds
perching here daily,
blending
with the quiet lure of peace.

Take note of passersby,
of hurricanes that visit our city in Fall.

They have eaten Captain Dee's head,
flooded the Atlantic
with iron boxes
owned by Ahmed,
Tom,
Mickey,
Mina,
and Melba,
who dropped bombs,
chased away fishy boats and
stood side by side
as they pulled countless triggers
at our enemies.

To destroy,
not preserve,
their memory
is
to hang
my words outside

continued

with a category five hurricanes
in sight.

Don't leave innocent faces
in the path
of hurricane Katrina.

Return this space
to Indians.

Can you?

Muscular Soldier

Because of you
names inscribed on crossed sticks,
some hanging on marble,
have assembled in this quiet field
we assemble in, but never leave.
I tread upon tiny paths
stopping by each flagged tomb, to ask a comrade
why we stormed civilian homes in the east firing shots,
waded across the Atlantic
and mangled the dreams of school children

Because of you,
I ache from the allergies of spring.
I can't forget your arrogant,
shrewd,
fierce face,
your muscular arms and clenched teeth
when you open fire on tanks,
on school buses.

Because of you
I piss the blood
of a freedom fighter,
kiss oriental dreams goodbye
while my bride,
engaged to death,
dances in nightclubs
with drowsy soldiers.

Because of you
I walk the parks alone,
saluting armored statues
that have
no sight
and no voice.

When Marlene,
the oldest witch on our street
is asleep,
I stay on my porch
humming military songs,
watching the stars,
hoping one will drop
on my lap.

First Envoy

I come from the other sea.
They call me seagull
because I swim through the moon
and perch on trees in the dark.

I know the seer
who wrote dead folks' names
on a scroll,
dumped it into the river
and
watched it
sail toward the sea.

He had seen their fate in a glass jar--
those who collapsed from armchairs
and never spoke again,
those who fell off Pan Am and
TWA
whose parts splattered across Lockerbie.

Their tender souls linger in the fuselage
waiting for the call.

I'll never enter an aircraft again.

The bridge I have crossed
is the gulf between life and me.
There are no planks and no iron here.

But God
can bring you here
where
I munch ants,

continued

dance with reptiles,
tour the world
in seconds,
and dine
with dead faces from
Malaysia,
Botswana,
Kalamazoo,
Dublin,
Aruba,
Buenos Aires.

Second Envoy

I come back to this
forlorn fortress
where Danny and Kaka grew,
to eat crumbs
abandoned for the birds,
perchance to sleep until dawn.

I see my face on a black-white photo
smiling back at me.

Janice,
your earrings and smile
still are golden.

Your turgid buttocks
and plump cheeks
are ready for my soft lips.

Your sautéed chicken
simmers on the table.
Sweaty,
red wine is ready
to fill the glass,
while D & K
rehearse sweet sounds
for Jesus.

Can you see me?
Can you feel me?
Can you drink my breath?

Before I return above,
I will perch on our bed

continued

and purge
my soul of the bomb
that silenced my breath
and exiled my flesh
to the land
of whispers
and faceless faces.

Come.
Take
my hand.

Stranger in the House

The land of no return
occupied rooms and gaping hostels:
is paved with roses and seaweeds.

Is it for its scintillating beauty
that we don't hasten to go there?

Is it for the choirs that incessantly
sing the tenor and high pitch?

Is it for the violins,
drums,
tambourines,
Beethoven and
Dolly Parton
with Gabriel
at the helm?

Is it
for the doves that
s
a
i
l
the skies,
the white-winged angels
with joyous smiles
floating everywhere,
perching in the hostels?

Or
for
me?

continued

Is it that dad,
Mr. T.
and Queenie,
who left
decades ago?

Even Methuselah
has never returned
to the US
to describe God's face?

For God and Country

I must pack up
a whistling gun,
brush, toothpaste,
juice and water,
t-shirts and sweaters
and row off the harbor,
jostle through rustling waves,
swelling waters,
swirling sights,
unfazed by whales and crocodiles
to your borders.

I'll tan and bathe,
sleep
and
awake near the Suez Canal.

My beard
will reach my shins
and
I'll waft up the way
and camp
among clouds,
twilight,
dawn,
and
high noon
to see
God's face.

Allah!!!!!

continued

I,
too
am,
America.

For Country and God?

I can't just
stand here
watching
so many marine hats
sardined on one deck
enjoy seeing new regions.

My Sunday school students
are waiting for me.

Their parents
have dropped them
by the church door
and
left
in their Mercedes Benz.

The children,
our turbo,
are singing
the Halleluiah,
clapping
their feeble hands,
stamping
their feet.

America.
France.
Germany.
England.
Japan.
Canada.
Russia.
Italy.

continued

Are
your
children
in
that
choir?

The Politician at Camp

Build your tents.
Dig deeper holes.
Mount
larger sand bags
atop the wall.

Dig
countless wells.
Cram Tutsi.
Learn Pidgin.
Learn English.
Eat Mandarin.
Speak Japanese.
Read Sanskrit.

They have built
farm-to-market
roads.

Drop
that
gun.

Open
your
stores
and
let in
their
goods.

The Ultimate Diplomat

Sheikh!
Seminarian!
Monk
Dalai Lama
Those bodies
will decay
Unexhumed.

I
have
come
here
many
times.

I
have prayed
with the Chaplain
hoping
t
h
e
s
e
bodies,
clad
in
international uniforms,
would wake up
and return
to their families.

Politician
Glaxo Unwelcome.

Stop
the
wars!

About the Author

Dr. Ngwainmbi's publishing history spans three decades. His writings have been described as "intriguing", "mystical", "outstanding," "magical", "brings a breath of fresh air", "vivid", with "good riveting imagery", "very powerful", "poetry for justice and peace". Pulitzer prize-winning poet, Gwendolyn Brooks, has said his "poems have…fierce urgency. Serious mischief is cleverly combined."

He is considered a distinguished scholar on the use of communication technology for grassroots development and strategic capacity building, including development of human capital in the Third World. Recently, he signed contracts for two books—a collection of essays by minority professors across US universities and a memoir-- to be published by Edwin Mellen Press. Recently, he published a groundbreaking article in *Handbook of Black Studies* and another in *Diverse* (formerly *Black Issues in Higher Education*. He has been invited to contribute material for the production of the *Encyclopedia of African Religions* which will be published by Sage.

Dr. Ngwainmbi has authored ten books & numerous articles, some in refereed journals. He has received scholarly awards and critical acclaim for four poetry collections, *A Bush of Voices, Shackles on a Ghost Skull, Sim's Poetic Column* and *Whispers on My Pillow*. The most widely critiqued poems include "Standing by a Black Corpse" in *African News Digest*, "Nelson Mandela" in *the Continent*, "The People Who Cried We Are" in *African Mirror*, "The Lawn Mower" and "Last Night" in *Electric Acorn*. Also widely read are *Communication Efficiency and Rural Development in Africa* and *Exporting Communication Technology to Developing Countries*—both dealing with development issues. Reviews appear in the *Library Journal*, newspapers and online, including Amazon, Yahoo, Barnes& Noble, Univpress, Apples and Oranges.com. My works are translated into French, Spanish and Afrikaans. Reviews have appeared in the *Daily Advance, 2001-2002, Virginia Pilot, West Africa Magazine, Blue & White Flash* (Mississippi), Univpress. com, Apples & Oranges.com. Barnes & Noble amazon.com, *Morgan Mirror, Drumbeat, Jackson Daily News; Daily Mississippian, Soundings, Electric Acorn,* (Ireland), *Daily Advance, and The Virginian Pilot*. He is the featured poet in *Poesia* (October, 2006). See www.indianbaypress.com Feb. 2006 newsletter.

His poetry credits include ten books and scores of publications in literary magazines, anthologies, and newspapers. Top among them are found in the following anthologies: **Immigration, Emigration, Diversity** (Chapel Hill Press); *Wilderness House Literary Review, The Washington Review*; *New Poets from West Africa* (anthology); *The New African Poetry* edited by Tanure Ojaide & T. Sallah. (Lynne Rienner Publishers); *Symphony of Verse; New Poets of West Africa* (Malthouse Press, Nigeria); *Janus; La Colombe. New Horizons.* (Yaoundé University Press). *The Mould* (Yaoundé University Press-Cameroon), *New Directions: The Howard University Magazine, Sensations Magazine, www.whlreview.com* and *Indian Bay Press.*

Published commentary on his poetry come from Archbishop Desmond Tutu, Prof. Blyden Jackson, Dr. R. Wright, Drs S. Nyang; T. Sallah (author & poet), G. Remsen (Broadcaster, WHAT Radio Station (Philadelphia); and award-winning literary figures like Jaki Shelton Green and J. Douglas Stuber.

He was recently invited by Emmy Award-winning broadcaster, Ed Gordon, to discuss cultural conflicts on the National Public Radio.

Emmanuel K. Ngwainmbi (pseudo. Sim E. Kombem) earned the doctorate in Communication from Howard University, Masters and Bachelor degrees in English & Literature from Jackson State and Yaoundé Universities, respectively. He is full Professor, Director of International Programs and former Chairperson in the Department of Language, Literature & Communication at Elizabeth City State University, North Carolina.

Dr. Ngwainmbi has served on a number of local, national and foreign academic boards, including the National Association of African American Studies & Affiliates and *The Journal of Black Studies*. The recipient of many academic awards including the Distinguished International Scholar Award from the Chinese Academy for Social Sciences, Departmental Teacher of the Year, and a three-time inductee in *Who's Who Among America's Teachers* ©, he has lectured and read widely in the US, Europe, Asia and Africa. He has been a guest on Voice of America; October Gallerylive.com; the British Broadcasting Service-Africa (BBC); WRVS 89.9 FM-N. Carolina; WJSU FM 88-Mississippi; WPFW 89.8 FM-Washington, DC; TV Channel 16-Cable Washington, D.C.; Associated Writers Conference, 29th Annual Conference Program Guide-Virginia; national and provincial radio stations in Cameroon; Martin Luther King, Jr. Library-Washington, DC, and Chapel Hill.

Through his writings, he hopes to raise awareness regarding world peace and African customs. He lives in Elizabeth City, North Carolina.